CODE

The Tower of Glass

Janice Pimm ◗ **Jon Stuart**

Galactic Orbit

D1344965

Contents

OXFORD

UNIVERSITY PRESS

Macro Marvel
(billionaire inventor)

Welcome to Micro World!

Macro Marvel invented Micro World – a micro-sized theme park where you have to shrink to get in.

A computer called **CODE** controls Micro World and all the robots inside – MITEs and BITEs.

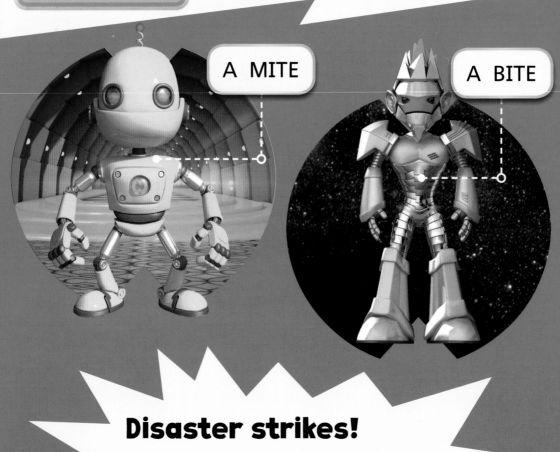

A MITE

A BITE

Disaster strikes!

CODE goes wrong on opening day.
CODE wants to shrink the world.

Macro Marvel is trapped inside the park …

Enter Team X!

Four micro agents – *Max, Cat, Ant* and *Tiger* – are sent to rescue Macro Marvel and defeat CODE.

Mini Marvel joins Team X.

Mini Marvel
(Macro's daughter)

In the last book ...

- Max and Tiger got stuck in a pit.
- Cat rescued Max and Tiger but the jets returned!
- Cat went micro-size and tricked the jets. They are safe ... for now!

**CODE key
(1 collected)**

You are in the Galactic Orbit zone.

3

Before you read

Sound checker
Say the sounds.

ow   oi

Sound spotter
Blend the sounds.

oi	l

s	oi	l

t	ow	er

f	l	ow	er	s

Tricky words
was
he
you
they

Into the zone

Team X and Mini go to the red planet. What do you think it will be like?

4

The Red Planet

The rocket was at the red planet.
Ant got off to look. He took snaps.

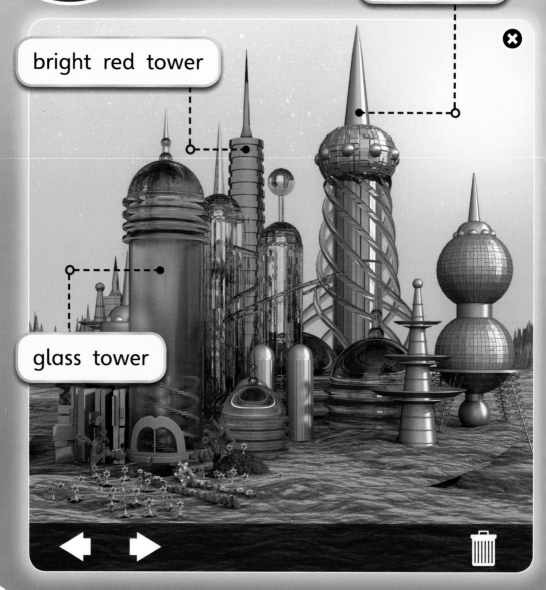

You can see lots of towers.

silver tower

bright red tower

glass tower

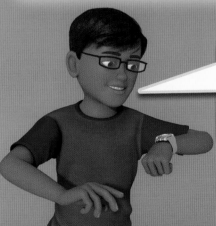

Look at the MITEs.
They polish the towers
and dig the gardens.

The MITEs plant flowers in the red soil.

The planet is boiling hot. The showers keep the flowers wet.

Look!
The MITEs fill the jets with oil.
Is the BITE on this planet?

Now you have read ...
The Red Planet

Text checker
What did Ant take snaps of?

MITE fun
Imagine you are on the red planet.
What would you see?
What would it feel like?
What would you hear?

Do you like
the red planet?

11

Before you read

Sound checker
Say the sounds.

ow   **oi**

Sound spotter
Blend the sounds.

d	ow	n

sh	ow	er

t	r	ow	e	l

b	oi	l	i	ng

Tricky words
be
are
he
they

Into the zone
This story is called 'A Trap'.
What do you think the trap
might be?

A Trap

Team X and Mini must get the CODE key from the BITE.

Tiger's watch is flashing.
The BITE must be near.

Tiger and Mini shrink. Now
the BITE will not see them.

It is boiling hot.
The towers are a long way off.

Tiger puts on his bounce boots.
Now he can jump high and fast.

They see the MITEs digging the soil.

The MITE digs the soil and lifts up Tiger and Mini!

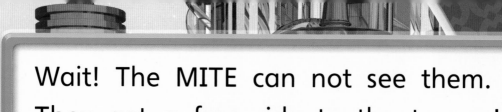

Wait! The MITE can not see them. They get a free ride to the towers!

The MITE puts down the trowel.
Tiger and Mini jump down.

They go into the tower.
They can not see the BITE.

The door shuts.
It is a trap!
How can they get out now?

Now you have read ...
A Trap

Text checker
Why did Tiger's watch flash?

MITE fun
Look back at the story.
Can you retell it using the pictures?

OXFORD
UNIVERSITY PRESS

Great Clarendon Street, Oxford, OX2 6DP,
United Kingdom

Oxford University Press is a department of the University of Oxford.
It furthers the University's objective of excellence in research, scholarship,
and education by publishing worldwide. Oxford is a registered trade mark of
Oxford University Press in the UK and in certain other countries

British Library Cataloguing in Publication Data
Data available

978-0-19-834006-5

9 10

Paper used in the production of this book is a natural, recyclable product
made from wood grown in sustainable forests. The manufacturing process conforms
to the environmental regulations of the country of origin.

Printed in China by Hing Yip

Acknowledgements
Character illustrations by Jonatronix Ltd, Senior Art Director: Jon Stuart, 3D artist: Sean Frisby
Series editors: Maureen Lewis, Di Hatchett
Phonics consultant: Marilyn Joyce
Teaching notes written by Rachael Sutherland
Project X concept by Rod Theodorou and Emma Lynch

Will Tiger and Mini escape?

Now you need to read
Flight of Fear.

Project X

Book Band 3
Yellow

Oxford
Level 3

Letters and Sounds
Phases 2 and 3
Focus GPCs: ow (/ou/),
oi (/oi/)
Tricky words: was, he,
you, they, be, are

CODE
7

Team X face their biggest
challenge yet ... to battle the BITEs,
rescue Macro Marvel and stop CODE!

The Red Planet
Team X and Mini are on the red planet.
Ant snaps the sights.

A Trap
Tiger and Mini go to the towers.
Will the BITE see them?

OXFORD
UNIVERSITY PRESS

How to get in touch:
web   www.oxfordprimary.co.uk
email schools.enquiries.uk@oup.com
tel.   +44 (0) 1536 452610
fax   +44 (0) 1865 313472

ISBN 978-0-19-
9 780198 340065

CODE

2

Cat's Quest

Alison Hawes
Jon Stuart

OXFORD

In this book

Focus GPCs
* x, y, qu

Tricky words
* was, you, my

Team X words
* Tiger, shrink, BITE

See **Project X CODE** Teaching and Assessment Handbook 1 (Yellow–Orange) for detailed session notes.

Reading check

* Before reading, check that children know the meaning of less familiar words:

   ### In a Fix
   fix – a tricky situation

   ### Stuck Fast!
   quest – a long and difficult search to find or get something

* During reading, check that children can recall the GPCs x, y, qu and use this knowledge to blend and read words in the story, e.g. six, yells, quit.